A LAYMAN'S
UNDERSTANDING
OF THE
BOOK OF REVELATION!

A LAYMAN'S UNDERSTANDING OF THE BOOK OF REVELATION!

Place The Island Of Patmos

Alan Shinkfield

Copyright © 2021 Alan Shinkfield.

All rights reserved. No part of this book may be reproduced in any form or by any electronic or mechanical means, including information storage and retrieval systems, without permission in writing from the publisher, except by reviewers, who may quote brief passages in a review.

ISBN: 978-1-63795-421-8 (Paperback Edition)
ISBN: 978-1-63795-422-5 (Hardcover Edition)
ISBN: 978-1-63795-420-1 (E-book Edition)

Scripture taken from Holy Bible, New International Version®, NIV® Copyright ©1973, 1978, 1984, 2011 by Biblica, Inc.® Used by permission. All rights reserved worldwide.

Book Ordering Information

Phone Number: 315 288-7939 ext. 1000 or 347-901-4920
Email: info@globalsummithouse.com
Global Summit House
www.globalsummithouse.com

Printed in the United States of America

CONTENTS

Chapter 1 – Introduction! 1
Chapter 2 – Letters To The Churches In Asia Minor 9
Chapter 3 – The Horses To Be Loosed 13
Chapter 4 – Two Deaths – One Resurrection! 17
Chapter 5 – John Was Chosen, Why? 21
Chapter 6 – The Trumpets 25
Chapter 7 – Towards End Times 31

Summary 35
Epilogue: Invitation And Warning 39

CHAPTER ONE

INTRODUCTION!

Revelation chapter one verse three:-

Blessed is the one who reads the words of this prophesy, and blessed are those who hear it and take to heart what is written in it, because the time is near.

Revelation chapter 22, verses 18 &19 :-

I warn everyone who hears the words of the prophesy of this book; if anyone adds anything to them, God will add to him the plagues described in this book. And if anyone takes words away from this book of prophesy, God will take away from him his share in the tree of life and in the holy city, which is described in this book.

Why should a layman be more able to understand revelation than learned students and leaders in the Christian Church today? Mainly because he is not persuaded by others before him, and because of everything in the world, common sense has been replaced by learning.

What is learning? It is the study of theists handed down from one learned person to another, on the other hand wisdom is a true and wonderful gift from God. Proof! Consider Solomon who sought and gained wisdom and built magnificent gardens, orchards, could harden pure gold and was noted in the then world as all knowing.

The greatest problem with learning is that if an error is made in translating or the continuance of passing that on through future generations, that error is not corrected and possibly expanded and lead to mistakes for believers of generation of future seekers. As wisdom is a gift from God and He is truth, when honesty and fully dispensed by man, there can be no mistaken adoption of that message.

Man has no true conception of God, we are told in the Holy Book that we were made in His image, which I believe must mean physical and spiritual. For we are told that He walked with Adam and Eve in the garden of Eden in the cool of the evening.

Physically, Genesis Chapter 3 verse 8;
Spiritually John's Gospel Chapter 4 verses 23 & 24.

So we should be left with no doubt that there are two distinct worlds for all men.

There are many and varied misconceptions, mainly issuing from man's fertile reasoning yet we still find the truth misinterpreted. The fact that we recognise God as an old man with white hair and a beard and a sturdy staff, this denies our Christian belief in eternity. If eternity is forever, should we assume that the God who created the world and all that is in it, has never aged, and remains as He was, is and ever shall be.

We can now be confident that the staffs of Moses and Aaron had the blessing of special powers. Aaron's staff becoming a snake before Pharaoh,

Exodus Chapter 7 verses 8 & 9.

Moses & Aaron, a rock and water.

Numbers Chapter 20 verses 9 to 11.

Perhaps this has become the reasoning for God to have a staff as depicted in paintings and in our mental vision of Him. God has no need for a staff to preform what we declare as miracles, nor to assist Him in His every day activities. As the ancient master painter showed us that angels had wings, but did they?

When Michael lead the army of God against Satan's revolution, would they have proved more of a hindrance rather than an asset.

Revelation Chapter 12 verse 7.

The more we ponder, the less we know, but when we accept that the Bible was written so many years ago, surely as the world changes we must consider some changes would have transpired that show that heaven was a place where things of earth can exist.

Would God deny to His faithful in Paradise any of the true and real pleasures that we know and enjoy in his world. The fruit, the birds, the flowers, all those things that when we open eyes we will see God.

There is a difference, in heaven all things act to the glory of God and to fulfil those promises made to His people throughout the Bible. On earth man's fierce desire for power, lust for material objects will see such wonderful gifts used for improper and immoral interests.

We are blessed with modern day transport, why would angels need wings, and when we consider UFO's are sighted flying around, why is it not considered that these are a part of God's reconnaissance and keep Him aware of the predicament man's high opinion of his self worth, has brought this, once a gem in God's overall plan to the state of evil we witness every day.

The Four Living Creatures!

Revelation Chapter 4 verses 6 to 9.

It would be very interesting to seek from the science fiction writers how and for what purpose these creatures fulfilled. They would possibly interpret the, as being seen in a Doctor Who episode, I do believe that they had a purpose rather than just praising God. Their faces translated into the meaning behind these faces would be as such; Lion, king of the beasts ruler; the Ox, strength, Man intelligence, the Eagle, without doubt, flight.

As well as the faces each had six wings, presumably for flight, and covered with eyes, all these were for a reason. In modern day technology, we could suppose that instead of eyes, these were cameras which as these travelled they could transmit signals back to a colossal monitor, keeping all heaven abreast and informed of the trials, turmoil and degradation of what was once an earthly paradise. One of the benefits of being a layman is that I am not bound by any doctrine or man made church laws.

The Holy City, the New Jerusalem.
Revelation Chapter 21 verses 1 to 4.

The Chosen People.

Deuteronomy Chapter 14 verse 2.
Exodus Chapter 19 verse 5.
Genesis Chapter 17 verse 7.

I would ask you to ponder this, in Revelation there is no doubt that a New Jerusalem will be established and a new order furnished for the world and its saved people. The New Jerusalem is coming down from the heavenly kingdom and what is visible is the new Arc of the New covenanter, the saving Blood of Jesus Christ.

There is also no doubt that the Hebrew race are the chosen people of God, then comes the big but, when the truth of the Messiah was denied to the people, Paul's conversion opened up the borders of the chosen and included the Gentiles of every colour, creed, and nation. God did place restrictions on which section was a worship area for the Jews, and that the gentiles would be restricted to the gentiles area.

Could it be that the New Jerusalem is the habitation of a body of the Jesus people with the mark of Christ on their hands or foreheads, whose names are in the Book of Life. We associate the word church as being a building but it is not, for a building is a material object, not able to operate unless it is powered by men and women of like minds and fully dedicated to the God of all creation.

So we find that the Church (building), needs human hands, bodies, minds under the direction of the Holy Spirit to prove successful for the tasks each of us was ordained. This then means that the true church is a group of people called to the glory of God and the extension of His earthly Kingdom.

As Revelation is quoted as a Book of Prophesy and referring to previous prophesies listed throughout the New Testament and I am quoting from Paul's Letters.

> *First Corinthians Chapter 12 verse 10.*
> *First Corinthians Chapter 14 verse 3.*
> *First Corinthians Chapter 14 verse 31.*

From these readings we can be assured that prophesy has been a part of Christian enlightenment. Yet we adhere to other gifts mentioned, wisdom, knowledge, faith, healing, recognising spirits, speaking in tongues, interpretation of those tongues, as prophesies are given they are quickly clouded by doubt and religious convictions.

It would seem that such gifts are used many times in ways which are not congruent with Biblical teachings. Such gifts have become a source in evil hands, as false prophets utilise such gifts for money.

Biblical Reference :-

Acts Chapter 8 verses 18 to 24.

As prophesy does not seem to be important in our present Christian life style, we can now know why the Book of Revelations not seamed of essential enough to read or even peruse, the reasons for this are because Revelation gives us many points to ponder, and there are many faithful Christians who have admitted to me they have never read Revelation and do not plan to embark on such a study.

The reasons vary from being too scary and not easily understood, and perhaps it shows God as a vengeful God and not as we envisage Him, but all these are unacceptable, and for confirmation read the Old Testament, when lessons were taught and blessings given.

If we only read the scripture that we like or appealed to our thinking our education would be grossly limited.

Revelation can only be accepted as extremely important when we earnestly accepted as being extremely important when we earnestly seek the true understanding through prayerful study.

CHAPTER TWO

LETTERS TO THE CHURCHES IN ASIA MINOR

Before embarking on this chapter, you are asked just what do you know about these churches? Positioned on Asia Minor, they received teaching from both Paul and John, remember John was exiled on a rocky island called Patros, for reasons that concerned John's teaching and ministering to these churches.

Honestly examine your worship centre, for no matter where you meet, what time day and night you meet, this is the most sacred time for you are standing before God and His heavenly hosts. Let us examine your worship centre, being very honest and admitting the ever present faults. How do you see your church, successful because of the numbers, the size of your centre, your bank balance of most importantly your involvement in the community.

Do as Jesus did and will do again, look outside your building, do you see a congregation which stands up for the oppressed, assists the less fortunate, is caring, loving and compassionate towards every one in the community, no matter what they believe? If not, you need to change. If one adult or child suffers in any way in your town or city, the number that worship in your centre are wasting their time, because you are not treading in the footsteps of the Master Jesus Christ.

Now read what Jesus found in these churches in Asia Minor, which were spiritually led at various times by John or Paul.

Revelation Chapter 2 Ephesus and Smyrna.

So Ephesus had some good points, their deeds, hard work, perseverance, they were against the wicked and tested the false prophets but their problem they had lost their first love. They were called to repentance. Does your church still have the fierce desire to do as Jesus did, or do you follow man's instituted laws or teaching?

Turning now to Smyrna, perhaps at the risk of coping the plagues as prophesied at the commencement of this book. I feel a minor change should be made to update this letter. Jesus warns about people calling themselves when they are not, In today's time we now find the name of Christian is used on people who are not of that persuasion. These are now bundled into the synagogue of Satan. The church was poor and suffered persecution even to the promise of prison. They were told to be faithful and receive the Crown of Life.

Revelation Chapter 2 Pergamum and Thyatira.

Even though Pergamum was a city of evil, scripture tells that it was where Satan had his throne, the believers remained true to Jesus and did not renounce their faith even though one of their number had been put to death. Those of evil intent were called upon to repent or suffer the consequences, but those who overcome will receive the rewards of manna and a white stone.

In Hydrating on the credit side they did good deeds, had love and faith, servitude and perseverance, on the minus side they allow a false prophet to mislead the people into immorality. The promise to the faithful that no other burdens will be placed upon them and they will receive authority over nations with an iron fist.

Revelation Chapter 3 Saudis and Philadelphia.

A warning to all denominations, the words of Jesus, 'I know your works, you are visibly alive on the inside of your worship chamber, but you are dead with your outreach to the many needing your compassion and comfort. Like Saudis you must wake up to your ordination, be fruitful, remember what you have received, obey and repent. Those few who have not renounced their God, they will be clothed in the pure white of the Saints.

Jesus knew the church in Philadelphia was of little strength, yet they held on to His words and did not deny His name. Our churches of today seem to be strong in numbers but very lacking in strength of honesty and good character. Again we are reminded of Satan's synagogue where the Jewish name has been falsely used and those who use or quote the Bible words are liars. If we gain nothing from this letter we must transpose the meaning to the modern day. Instead of Jews insert the name Christian and becomes apparent the present church is displaying an inward and not the desired outward presence needed to welcome Jesus the King back to reform the world.

Do any of these stories effect the thinking of your worship centre? They should you know, these are observation made by the Leader, whose words are honest and true. Do not make the mistake that there is not a message here for you both as an individual and a special group. Do you recognise that there a massive group of people looking for what you have and not getting the opportunity to find it. Don't be selfish, don't hog the good news, if it is rejected at least you tried, but don't forget to let God in on your plan, for His cooperation is not only needed but essential.

Revelation Chapter 3 Boadicea.

Jesus' words cannot be changed for they are printed from verse 14 to 19 and if have not got the message by then pray a little bit harder. These are the words of the Amen, the faithful and true witness, the ruler of God's creation. I know your deeds, that you are neither cold or hot. I wish you were one or the other! So, because you are lukewarm – neither hot or cold - I am about to spit you out of my mouth. You say I am rich; I have acquired wealth and do not need a thing. But you do not realise that you are retched, pitiful, poor, blind and naked. I counsel you to buy from me gold refined in the fire, so you can be rich, and white clothes to wear, so you can cover your shameful nakedness; and salve to put on your eyes, so you can see. Those whom I love I rebuke and discipline. So be earnest and repent.

The Master has spoken, listen as never before.

CHAPTER THREE

THE HORSES TO BE LOOSED

As a believer in the sacrifice of Jesus Christ on the cross, I know that he died for my sins, and now I am forgiven of all past, present and future sins. I can now no longer be judged as the price has been paid. Jesus accepted my guilt and the guilt of all humanity, we just have to accept His word and God's promise.

This rider and horse present the message clear and understandable but unless you have already accepted the sacrifice of God's only Son, be assured that this rider is coming to give you a final chance of salvation.

Being the only sinless person who ever lived as a man on earth, and was now in heaven, it befell Jesus to open the seven seals of the scroll.

The first seal disclosed a rider and a horse that was a chapter of prophesy, and again the visions explained were what John knew and of course was acquainted with, the horse as an instrument to forward messages over long distances, but today the horse would almost be obsolete, with telecommunications, and all modern communication systems

The first seal when opened revealed to John a white horse its rider equipped with a bow, the rider was given a crown, and rode out as a conqueror bent on making a conquest. Turning to my school dictionary, I find that conquest means to win the affection of a person, a person or thing conquered. You should be asking now what if the rider and horse have already been loosed in the world? This has given rise to the fact that I am an avid believer in a great and world wide Christian Revival. We have had so many why shouldn't we have yet another chance.

I see the importance of the rider and white horse being the first to go forth. We should pause here to examine that if my dictionary is correct, the horse and rider were given the power and ordered to conquer or win the affection over from we have, the world wide evil

Ask your self can you not see a world wide trend today of returning to the Christian Faith, and how these revivals are because of the ordination given to the rider and his mount the white horse. When the second seal was broken, John's vision was of a rider on a fiery red horse, the rider was equipped with a large sword. His mission to take peace from the earth, to set man against man and have them slaying each other.

This prophesy has been proven by the gang wars, racism, and the terrorism that stops a women being alone in the streets of a night. When wars commenced we knew who our enemy was but now with drug cartels, the laziness of people refusing to work and make a reasonable wage, but being tempted by Satan and his disciples to take the easy way no matter who it effected. It is now about man or woman against fellow men and women trying to enforce and dominate their views and ideas upon all others.

By now you should have your favourite newspaper in hand, (Silly me, I live in Country Queensland and we don't have a local paper any more). You may not compare John's writing to those of the journalists of today. We have the pandemic causing frustration and fear, is this an introduction to what is coming as promised in Revelation.

This prophesy has been promised and proven by terrorism and its new pathway against ordinary members of the community, happening in busy public areas by misguided people who believe they will eventually be unscathed. Remember there is a promised judgement after earthly death.

When the Lamb opened the third seal, John looked and there was a rider on a black horse, the rider held a pair of scales in his hand. This was Justice for a voice said, ' Two pounds of wheat for a days wages and six pound of barley for a days wages, and do not damage the oil and the wine. With the on growing war between management and workers, this rider could return any time now.

The fourth seal when broken brought forth a rider on a pale horse the rider's name was Death and Hades followed close behind. They were given power over a fourth of the earth to kill be the sword, famine and plague, and be the wild beasts of the earth.

The fifth seal John saw under the alter the souls of those had been slain because of the word of God. They called out in a loud voice, How long, Sovereign Lord, holy and true, until you judge the inhabitants of the earth and avenge our blood? Then each of them was given a white robe , and they were told to wait a little longer.

The breaking of the sixth seal introduced a mighty earthquake. The sun turned black like sackcloth made of goats hair, the whole moon turned blood red, and the stars in the sky fell to earth , as figs drop from a fig tree when shaken. People hid in caves and among rocks and called to the mountains and rocks, fall on us and hide us from the face of God and the wrath of Jesus.

Again as Christianity preaches love, compassion and peace there are forces preaching hate, domination of the weak and helpless, even to eventual death, and little is being done to curtail such an evil doctrine. Where as Christianity is finding intense criticism and opposition in every thing we try to do, but we should brace ourselves for the battle and follow our previously victorious leader, but I am afraid to write this but we do need fewer talkers and more doers following the footsteps of the Master.

We should be free and able to celebrate our Christian festivals Christmas and Easter as other religions celebrate theirs, without any comments and or supposed reasons for the ending of these times so important to those who love Good and His Son.

CHAPTER FOUR

TWO DEATHS – ONE RESURRECTION!

This is the reason that Revelation is not read, people do not understand and do not have the patience to study or look for answers. Accepting Jesus Christ as your Master and a willingness to research and learn, and without these you will never earn the name of Christian.

What does John write about death and resurrection?

Revelation Chapter 20 verses 4 to 6.

I saw thrones on which were seated those who had been given authority to judge. And, I saw the souls of those who had been beheaded because of the word of God. They had not worshipped the beast or his image and had not received his mark on their foreheads or hands. They came to life and reined with Christ for a thousand years. (The rest of the dead did not come to life until the thousand years were ended). This is the first resurrection. Blessed and holy are those who have a part in the first resurrection. The second death has no power over them, but they will be priests of God and of Christ and will reign with him for a thousand years.

I write this chapter on death and resurrection not because I am a theologian, or a student who has completed courses in understanding the truth of God's Word given in His Book the Bible. Rather it is because I truly believe that sometimes being to well educated on any one subject leaves no consideration for personal interpretation or understanding. There is one true ordination and that is the ordination by God or His Son, there can be no other, man does not have that power.

I also believe that although the meanings of scripture are not always clear and concise, there is a very good reason for this.

Jesus said in Luke Chapter 8 verses 9 & 10.

His disciples asked him what this parable meant. He said, 'the knowledge of the secrets of the Kingdom of God has been given to you, but to others I speak in parables, so that through seeing, they may not see, through hearing they may not understand.

Matthews view differs slightly, Chapter 13 -verse 10 to 13.

The disciples came to him and asked, 'Why do you speak to the people in parables?' He replied, ' The knowledge of the secrets of the kingdom of heaven has been given to you, but not to them. Whoever has will be given more, and he will have an abundance. Whoever does not have, even what he has will be taken from him. This is why I speak in parables.

Matthews Gospel Chapter 13 verses 34 & 35.

Jesus spoke all these things to the crowd in parables, he did not say anything to them without using a parable. So this was fulfilled what was spoken through the prophet Isaiah. 'I will open my mouth in parables. I will utter things hidden since the creation of the world.'

So in these three portions of scripture we have three instances as to why Jesus explained every thing he said was hidden in a different story or parable. This is the same reason that the Bible is not written to be understood by anyone who reads it. You have to prove it is not just a passing phase but a dedication by those wanting to find the truth of the world's history. People who seek wisdom from God and seek deeper meanings that can only be uncovered by study.

Before uncovering the hidden gems in this prophesy from Jesus to John, we must admit that all these parables were directed at the living conditions of the day. The trades of the day were preached and understood, The Sower and the Seed, The Wedding Feast, The Water into Wine, to people for whom these were all directed to, were a part of their every day life. Now over two thousand years into the future when now we have multi trades, how can we place past pieces into slots of today.

Today Christian must be adaptable and willing to search out the truth to find the real meaning. In other words, do some real labour to find the real interpretation of the words and the hidden gems. Dig up and find the precious Bible treasures hidden from the unbelievers eyes.

CHAPTER FIVE

JOHN WAS CHOSEN, WHY?

The Gospel Of John Chapter 1 verses 1 to 5'

John not only saw what the others saw, he was granted a wisdom to understand all that the others did not comprehend. Only John commences his works at the very beginning of creation and recognises Jesus as the Alpha and Omega and that Jesus was present at the beginning of heaven and earth. If he could believe and write this then he was the logical and perhaps the only choice to put to words the amazing visions he was about to witness.

John's Gospel Chapter 1 verse 1.
Revelation Chapter 22 verse 13.

Because of this, his first and last visions, he has an acceptance from Jesus, which enabled him to call himself, 'the disciple that Jesus loved!' I do not believe this was John's ego, for from the cross Jesus gave John to his mother and John to Mary as John her son.

John's Gospel Chapter 13 verses 22 & 23.

A further peruse it in,

John's Gospel Chapter 19 verses 26 & 27.

James D. Tabor poses the question was this John or could it be James, Jesus brother and the natural son of Mary? Again we have questions posed that have nothing to do what so ever with the ultimate sacrifice of Jesus on the cross and the real and true significance of purchased freedom from sin and eventual eternal life.

We can through Satan's forces be bogged down on insignificant questions and answers and loose precious time in going forth to spread the good news of forgiveness of yours and my sins. Great men and women of God have not always agreed on various points of doctrine and that is why we Christians are not united under the banner of Christ crucified.

Even after reading of the transfiguration we cannot accept that Jesus was a man, he could not have been God for God cannot abide with sin, so it was the man Jesus who was transformed, proof again that what Jesus suffered, he suffered as a man. If you have not already accepted this, do it now.

Revelation Chapter 22 verses 3,4,5.

Because of this attention to detail I wonder why John was not invited to witness the transfiguration. Was this because John had already accepted Jesus the Messiah who he was and his job description as Saviour for the believers of the past, present and future of all ages. I can only image that if John was a witness how the portrayal would have been written. But go back many things are hidden from not only our eyes but out understanding.

In dissecting the words that John wrote we must take into consideration that he would only have knowledge of where and when he lived and could not comprehend how things would change over a couple of centuries. John saw horses with metal armour, we would probably see tanks or armoured vehicles, the weapons of war of today. I have been told by an educated scholar that because of the difference between John's gospel and the writing in Revelation John could not of written Revelation because it was not his style.

Being reasonably uneducated, I prefer to use my common sense and admit that there is no way and no matter what was revealed to me could I foresee the world in another two thousand years. In comparing the two writings of John we find there is a difference in the writing, but also in the story.

The gospel was a record of living in reasonable surroundings, knowing the Master Jesus, the visions on Patios were spiritual and subjects John was not accustomed being introduced too. Revelation was just that a revelation of promises of things to come, John saw unimaginable things, that even at our stage of progression would find very hard to believe, but believe we must.

There is no doubt in my mind that because of his proven nature Jesus' compassion, love, and fellowship to his disciples had the reverse effect it had on them, of course they accepted and retuned what they were given, but each had proved in some way to have doubted, denied, betrayed, revenge as proved in Samaria. Sorry to mention this fact, but this is as our church is today, but the time is right and now to change as we ready ourselves for the tribulation as prophesied is upon us and we are still unready.

God knows us so well and John has record his vision prophesy into what he knew and understood, your mission and mine is to search and understand many of these visions. We must have that extremely close relationship with God and Jesus Christ that we will be led by the power of the Holy Spirit, we do not have to know all the details but be assured we are in close contact and union with THOSE who do know.

CHAPTER SIX

THE TRUMPETS

Revelation Chapter 8 verse 6.

Then the seven angels who had the seven trumpets prepared to sound them. Before embarking on these let us consider the pandemic as a plague effecting all the world's people, And to my fellow believers assure you that the mark of Jesus on your forehead or hands will exonerate you from these plagues. The ones receiving these promises will have the mark of the beast. Make sure that your family and friends are covered. I am trying to prove and assure you the time is near.

The first trumpet, brought Hail mixed with blood, and one third of the earth was burned up the trees, the green grass all burned up. Look at this section of scripture we are informed the even though these plagues were released as before in Egypt men's hearts will be hardened, they will curse God instead of the required repentance sought by God through His Son Jesus Christ.

The second angel's trumpet sounded and brought a huge blazing mountain that was thrown into the sea. A third of the sea turned to blood the same amount of sea creatures died and a third of the ships were destroyed.

The third trumpet and a great blazing star named Wormwood fell from the sky and a third of the rivers and springs turned bitter, and people died from these waters.

The fourth trumpet sound brought havoc in the sky again one third of the Sun, Moon and Stars were struck and turned dark, meaning a third of day and night were deprived of light, John then watched and heard an eagle cry out in a loud voice, Woe! Woe! Woe to the inhabitants on the earth, because of the trumpet blasts from the other three angels!'.

I will leave the reading from this chapter to you the reader except for quoting verse 4. They were told not to harm the grass of the earth or any plant or tree, but only those who did not have the seal of God on their foreheads.

Now we have to accept a few facts which I believe could be hidden to many, but not those who have received the gift of understanding Satan, an angel a Star with a key, the abyss and as I see Satan as an angel. By this reasoning he could be a material object, perhaps man. Lets what go back to school and recognise what are real objects and things the are in our minds because we have thought about them..

We are told the the star had a key, fitly we can establish this key is real and we are told it is for a particular place. The Abyss which is also real.

We now have to turn to :-
Revelation Chapter 20.
The thousand Years and the Judgement of Satan.

Please read this portion of chapter 20 for yourself, I just want you to accept the possibility that Satan is real and alive and is treated as a person and object. There is an angel coming down from heaven with two real and material things, a key and a great chain. He seized a real and living thing, the dragon, the ancient serpent the devil or Satan, come on now you cannot mistake who John is speaking about. The angel bound him for a thousand years and threw him into the Abyss, which is also real and a object, the angel then locked and sealed it over him.

From this we hat can we assume about Satan. We know he was an angel probably in charge of music. He was not as the ancient artist and he is depicted in some cases today, he did not have horns and hoofs and was not red, but pleasant to the eye, and had the number 666. We also know the the number of man is 7 so he was unrecognisable, to any who meet him and are beguiled and tempted and you do not recognise him why would buy his wares? Because he knows just what can destroy man's faith in goodness and righteousness. Money, sexual perversion, hate, power, bashings, whereas once killings and murders were a minority, now every weekend there are reports covering this and violent rapes. Has man deteriorated so far that morals mean nothing, or is it that Satan now owns his sway and stead of being led by normality we allow Satan to own our every thoughts and action. Now is the time to stop, life can be a whole lot better.

Have you reread chapter 20 of Revelation? Have you not now understood that a spirit can not held chained and locked and sealed for one thousand years. Does the thought arise in your mind the Satan is and was an angel, but was denied a spiritual form?

John then saw Thrones in which were seated those given authority to judge, I presume these were from those who cried out when Sovereign Lord when will we be avenged and were given white robes and told to wait just a little longer for more were coming. To a human mind their reward will be passing judgement on their prosecutors.

THE JUDGEMENT OF SATAN.

Revelation *Chapter 20 from verse 7.*

If Revelation is a book of prophesy, I truly wonder why along with the complete story included, why was the Rapture not even mentioned in Revelation?. Did it sound like a good idea, and was clasped upon for some hope? We read of a form of resurrection in two Gospels.

Matthews Gospel Chapter 24 verses 40 & 41.

"Two men will be in the field; one will be taken and the other left. Two women will be grinding with a hand mill; one will be taken and the other left.'

Luke's Gospel Chapter 17 verses 34 & 35.'I will tell you, on that night two people will be in one bed, one will be taken and the other left. Two women will be grinding grain together, one will be taken and the other left..'

If you have a wondering mind why so explicit to note they

were grinding with a hand mill?

As it seems with our beliefs when one has an opinion on a subject it does not take long before someone comes up with a theory that disproves the original. The Rapture is one of these. There are some views that believe that evil was destroyed on both Noah's flood, and the destruction of Sodom's evil, the Rapture would take evil ones not believers.

In the preceding verses 26 to 29 of Luke we are drawn to the days of Noah, when normal life was being practised and then the flood came and destroyed all but a favoured few. The story of Sodom is also recorded, that after Lot left, fire and sulphur rained down from heaven and destroyed them all.

When deep and serious thoughts are used, this would mean that the evil would be taken and the Christ filled would be left to suffer the plagues of the Tribulation.

We do place to much emphasis on debatable facts in the scriptures and not enough time looking at the personalities of those close to Jesus. It does not matter what station in life you attain, Would you wish to associate with fishermen, shepherds, tent makers, and persevere with them as they in their deepest hearts spoke without thinking. Jesus Christ did, so go use the talents you have been given and do likewise. GOD WILL ACCOMPANY YOU AND BLESS YOU.

CHAPTER SEVEN

TOWARDS END TIMES

Revelation Chapter 21 & 22.

As we approached these End Times of elation for believers in One Living God and therefore Salvation through the sacrifice of Jesus Christ His only Son, and to read foretaste of the horror to follow for those who have chosen to follow the evil one and wear his mark as his disciples.

In these times Satan will be at his busiest, recruiting the unsuspecting talents of those who will fall to his promises of power, position, excesses of riches, even fame to destroy any credence to the truth of goodness in God's full loving forgiveness.

People will suffer blindness and deafness to the inevitable, as the daily news reveals stories of wars, rumours of wars, man's desire to hurt, maim and even kill his fellow humans. But and from John's Visions of the plagues Satan's rewards are stronger than the promise of peace through God. May I Quote :- If a promise is to good to be true – it needs honest questioning.

With much promised We have in a few chapters many prophesies that must be fulfilled before the second coming of Christ Jesus, some causing fear and terror into those followers of the beast, but relief and peace to the followers of the Lamb without blemish. How can we educate non believers when they will not accept the Bible's history? I cannot impart to people of this age when they were never informed of a totally different

way of understanding, I cannot tell them of the plague set upon Pharaoh and Egypt to release the Jewish Nation as one from years of slavery. If they cannot accept this they will not envisage the horror of the world as it enters the time of tribulation.

The problem now is that in preaching the tribulation we do not offer the great and wonderful things as promised by both God and Jesus Christ, both of whom are noted for their truth through the ages. If you have not read Revelation you are missing out on a scripture that will calm your heart and fulfil your dream of future peace.

Revelation Chapter 21 verses 3 & 4.

And I heard a loud voice from the throne saying, 'Look! God's dwelling place is now among the people, and he will dwell with them. They will be his people, and God himself will be with them and be their God. He will wipe every tear from their eyes. There will be no more more death, or mourning or crying or pain, for the old order of things has passed away.'

We have waited for this time since the first bite of an apple, but do not forget the anguish that the Trinity suffered waiting for this moment. Do you consider for one moment that a God of love has not wanted to dwell with his beloved people? I trust that I have wet your appetites to read further chapters 21, and 22. and consider what you will receive just by changing and accepting God as the creator and Jesus Christ as your Saviour.

My warning to those following Satan, the beast, the devil, try to remove his mark, have no doubt we are many prepared to help and assist you find true life and gain the promises offered.

Revelation Chapter21 verse10.

The New Jerusalem, the Bride of the Lamb.

And he carried me away in the Spirit to a mountain great and high, and showed me the Holy City, Jerusalem, coming down out of heaven from God. Can we pause just for one minute, read that again, and yet God's word was changed by puny man and suggested they could make Jerusalem the Capital on Israel. This was God's gift to the new and better world. AMEN.

Has any one ever told you that there are two covenants from God, one in the Old Testament and one in the New Testament.

Both concern sacrifices the original sought sacrifices of animals, birds, grain, produce or wine,. The new concerned the only sinless man ever to walk on our earth, Jesus Christ Son of God. This covenant only asked for recognition of the

Messiah and the crucified Christ who gave all for you and me, believe this and be saved.

I write this chapter and I am saddened as I see young children with beautiful hearts and minds being corrupted and virtually destroyed by illegitimate parents either to busy or otherwise engaged and have not the time or inclination to introduce some Christian education into these young lives. We adults can close our eyes to the End Times but even the Bible tells us the the world will wear out. My sadness is caused by seeing friends relations, even acquaintances suffering the prescribed traumas and plagues set out so clearly before us.

WHO SHOULDYOU BE PRAYING FOR?

Throughout the Bible God has shown no harsh judgements against any one who offered their live to serve any of God's plans. I n the book of Joshua he used Rehab who was a prostitute, she saved Joshua's spies and was rewarded. May I ask what have you done against the Lord? Do you think that God has written you off, he would never do that because whereas you may not believe in him he does have faith in you, TRY HIM!

Some personal History as a young lad before I met Jesus, I listened to older boys and did things that I now know were wrong. It gave Satan a toe hold which he increased to a foot hold, and seventy years later he still uses the same plan of attack that I yielded too then. I can overcome but the mental anguish in my thought process some times can be devastating. Although I serve my Lord that wonderful peace that passes all understanding, sometimes I loose., but really although therein victory it comes at a price. From this please consider honestly is what you doing benefiting any one or causing concern or harm.

THE LORD BE WITH YOU!

SUMMARY

Now comes the hardest part putting experiences to Revelation, but to put plainly Daniel is an earlier edition.

The Jews were exiled again, this time in Babylon and Daniel sand his friend obeyed the law justly. With Hananiah, Mishel and Azariah and they were ordered to eat the king's designated food. But they refused and chose to eat vegetables and drink water, but their guard was afraid the would not be as the other slaves which would have displeased the king and cause trouble for their guard. However they looked fitter than the others.

Daniel was able to interpret dreams that the King had and this raised his position in Babylon. They also adhered to Jewish Law rather than proclamations from the king. The King raised Daniel to a very high position and renamed his companions. Hannah became Drachma, Michel, Me shah, and Ariah, Begone. This done on the orders of King Nebuchadnezzar. I believe you should read Daniels' story yourselves as there are a couple of important inter matching facts in both books Daniels and Revelation.

Daniel is truly blessed and continues to stand up for his God, they suffer a furnace, **Daniel Chapter 3 verses 13 to 24. Daniel in the den of lions. Daniel Chapter 6 verses 6 to 11.** Daniel's life continues as he is further blessed and continued to interpret dreams and visions.

Revelation confirms just what Daniel believed and lives, here promises are made which many doubt, but were proven in Daniel's Book no one is going to get a free ride to salvation and eternal life, we all have to contribute by becoming disciples for Christ. You may ask how. A servant or slave does not ask his master what is next, he is told and does it. Have you forgotten your days in the work force, you receive recompense for what you labour, back to the horses and the one with the scales, justice is coming.

The Next page is very important!
There is one factor of Revelation I have not covered, it is so important for you understanding.

Revelation Chapter 11 verses 3 to 13.

The Two Witnesses.

For the first time we are given an accurate vision of what happens when The truth is gives to the people. We have been very interested in who they are and its not recorded what they said. Like all practising Christians they would have preached the truth and by the abuse they received in return, the people are as yet not interested.

Verse Ten :-The inhabitants of the earth will gloat over them and will celebrate by sending each other gifts, because these two prophets had tormented those who live on the earth.

These witnesses after three and a half days the breath of life from God will enter them and they stood on their feet, and terror struck those who saw them. Then they heard a loud voice from heaven saying to them, " Come up Here." And they went up to heaven in a cloud, while their enemies

EPILOGUE: INVITATION AND WARNING

REVELATION CHAPTER 22 verses 12 to 16.

Look, I am coming soon! My reward is with me, and I will give to each person according to what they have done. I am the Alpha and the Omega, the First and the Last, the Beginning and the End.

Blessed are those who wash their robes, that they may have the right to the tree of life and may go through the gates into the city. Outside are the dogs, those who practice magic arts, the sexually immoral, the murderers, the idolaters and every one who practices falsehood. I, Jesus, have sent my angel to give you this testimony for the churches. "I am the root and the Offspring of David, and the bright Morning Star."

'AMEN.'

NOW IS THE TIME TO DECIDE!

If God has touched your hearts by the HOLY SPIRIT, through this book, sermon, or personal Contact, and you wish to prayerfully and honestly repent of your past life and dedicate you new life to the Saviour and Great Shepherd of the Christian Flock, Jesus Christ the opportunity is yours to record the date and sign your pledge below.

FULL NAME.

On this day the _____ of _____ 20_____ .

I _____ have petitioned God through Jesus Christ, His only Son, my now Saviour and have set before him a repentant heart, asking for forgiveness of my sins past, present and future, and as Jesus gave His life for me, give my life to Him to use as He will. AMEN!

MY SIGNATURE :-

OUR PRAYER FOR YOU!

May God's Richest blessings welcome you into the loving arms of our Lord and Master Christ Jesus, and may true joy and peace remain with you and give you strength to do His bidding until He Comes with GLORY. AMEN

www.ingramcontent.com/pod-product-compliance
Lightning Source LLC
LaVergne TN
LVHW041551060526
838200LV00037B/1240